Athlepreneurs

8 Lessons from Athletes
to Start Your Business
as a Champion

Laura Brandes

Copyright © 2013 Laura Brandes

All rights reserved.

No part of this publication may be reproduced, stored in a retrieval system, or transmitted in any form or by any means without the written permission of the publisher. The information provided in this book does not constitute legal, tax or accounting advice, but is designed to provide general information relating to business and commerce. The content is not a substitute for obtaining the advice of a competent professional, for example a licensed attorney, law firm, accountant or financial adviser. In no event shall the author be liable for any loss of profits, revenue or contracts, loss of anticipated savings or any direct or indirect, damages, or any consequential losses or any other special, exemplary, punitive or any other monetary or other damages or liabilities arising out of or relating in any way this book, the materials on or accessible via it, or any advice given by interviewees on this book.

ISBN-10: 1493674684
ISBN-13: 978-1493674688

DEDICATION

To my beloved husband Rod,

and

to all athletes around the world. Your endless motivation to improve performance inspires me everyday. Your passion, strength, braveness, and confidence are a powerful source of motivation today and for the generations to come.

CONTENTS

	Acknowledgments	I
	Introduction	iii
1	Lesson 1- Feasibility Test: find the right business for you before stepping onto the field	1
2	Lesson 2 - Partnerships: Roles & Responsibilities Guide to be a golden team	12
3	Lesson 3 – Your Ideal Offer: products and services that score big every day	29
4	Lesson 4 – Your Ideal Customer: get to know whom you play for, and fill the arena with raving fans	43
5	Lesson 5 – Visual Identity: you will wear this uniform everyday, so make it right since the first game	53
6	Lesson 6 – Sales: break the record with business goals that are realistic, measurable and achievable	63
7	Lesson 7 – Marketing: The 12 Laps Calendar: make every month count	80
8	Lesson 8 – Business Plan: why you won't get to the finals without one	89

ACKNOWLEDGMENTS

This book would never been possible without the presence of each one of you in my life: my husband Rodney Schunck, eternal partner in all dreams and journeys; my beloved brother Mauricio Brandes, a brilliant guy with a big heart; and my parents Augusto and Liliana, who taught me the value of honesty above all.

A big thanks to the amazing athletes who took their time to talk to me and share their experiences with so much passion: Fabiola Molina, Nayara Figueira, and Lara Puglia Teixeira.

Thank you Alicia Dunams for coaching me during all the processes of my first book, Elizabeth Hamilton for the impressive knowledge on book business, Marie Grace Villegas to assure all tasks were on track, Susan Lin for offering great advices on how I could improve the text, and my friend Linda Sherwin for the precious support.

I couldn't thank more the beautiful, inspiring, and strong women in my life: Maria José Calomeno, Ines Serantes, Dolores Schunck, Adria Brandes, Cristina A. Brandes, Noelcir Soligo, Zilda Ferraresi, Leila Brandes, Aline Zendonadi, Claudia Rocco, Lilian Lopes, Paula Labruciano, Vera Lucia Ramos, Raquel Fernandes, Samantha Valle, Ana Bravo, Christine Stein, Ann-Katrin Stengel, Melina Hartmann, Claudia Manning, Ingrid Rubiano, Silvia Cruz, Mariana Pilizaro, Virginie Florvil, and Adriana Arenas. Also my dearest friends Mauricio Tejeda, Johannes Donath, and Juan Luis Osorio.

I am grateful for the all friends who shared their time and business experience, especially Martina Jahn, Marcelo Cabral, Luciana Lobato, Paula Haito, and Katerina Kraus.

And finally, I want to thank the entrepreneurs who inspired me and shared incredible knowledge: Caroline Frenette, Marie Forleo, Melissa Cassera, James Wedmore, Rob Hatch, Chris Guillebeau, Trevor Turbull, Lewis Howes and Sean Malarkey.

INTRODUCTION

Before we begin with the 8 lessons in this book, I want to take a few minutes to thank you—not only because you bought my book, but most of all because you are investing in yourself. Even if by this time you have only a business idea, you are on the right track; you are dedicating time to transforming your idea into a successful endeavor.

I am passionate about sports, all kinds of sports. I love to see how athletes can improve their performance by training harder, how they never give up, always believing they are capable of going faster, higher, farther. During the more than ten years that I have been working in the sports industry, I never saw a champion who said, "I didn't believe I was capable of that." Never.

That is why I use sports and athletes as inspiration in all chapters. Throughout this book, I want to help you think about your business the same way top athletes do. They all started with a dream and planned every step on their journey to winning the gold medal. They accomplished one task at a time and saw their dream become reality. Athletes don't train only their bodies to win gold medals. They use their minds and their hearts.

Successful ENTREPRENEURS are like elite ATHLETES. I call them ATHLEPRENEURS. They have clear goals and measure the results, are focused, and don't give up (after all, adversities are part of everyone's life). They train to win and believe they are capable of that. They never stop learning and improving, and they plan their movements, celebrate every victory, and inspire others.

This book will guide you through eight important areas of starting new businesses, with examples that are easy to understand and to immediately apply. You will discover that opening a small business does not need to be a complicated venture. It can—and should—be fun. When you have clarity about what you are doing and why you are doing it, all tasks begin to have a purpose, and you begin to see progress.

I want you to succeed. I wrote this book with the intention of giving you the confidence and clarity you need to start a business that will bring fulfillment to your life. I will show you how, in eight lessons, each packed with inspiring stories from amazing athletes. I have started successful businesses myself and helped several entrepreneurs to start and improve their businesses. The lessons below are also the result of my experience, and I want to share them with you now.

Lesson 1- Feasibility Test: to help you validate your business idea

Lesson 2 - Partnerships: to support you and your partners to work better as a team and achieve great results for the business

Lesson 3 – Your Ideal Offer: to help you successfully prepare the best product and/or services assortment

Lesson 4 – Your Ideal Customer: techniques to learn all about your clients' needs

Lesson 5 – Visual Identity: it is more than just the name and logo for your business. Build a strong identity that resonates for your audience

Lesson 6 – Sales: you will be guided to create goals that are realistic, measurable, and achievable

Lesson 7 – Marketing: The 12 Laps Calendar: every month is an opportunity to sell, and you won't waste any

Lesson 8 – Business Plan: your guide to help you make better decisions based on facts and numbers

Do the exercises from all the lessons and fill in the workbook. Then you will have your business plan ready when you finish reading the book.

The workbook is a free bonus, and you can download it here: athlepreneur.tv/workbook

So take action now. Let's start together on the journey to winning your gold medal in business!

"An athlete cannot run with money in his pockets. He must run with hope in his heart and dreams in his head."

—Emil Zátopek

(19 Sep 1922–22 Nov 2000)

Czech long-distance runner, nicknamed the "Czech Locomotive," considered to be one of the greatest runners of the 20th century.

3 gold medals at the 1952 Summer Olympics in Helsinki: 5km, 10km, and 42km, when he decided at the last minute to compete in the first marathon of his life.

LESSON 1

FEASIBILITY TEST

Find the right business for you before stepping onto the field

TEST 1

People usually ask me: I have a business idea, but how do I know if I am prepared to be a business owner?

I generally answer back that the first test is pretty simple. You must ask yourself: Am I passionate about my business idea?

I chose to quote Emil Zátopek to open this lesson because there is an important truth there. Just as an athlete cannot run with money in his or her pockets, you also cannot run a business if you are thinking about only money. But if you are so passionate about your business idea that you want to share it with the world, you honestly believe you can create positive change in other people's lives, then yes, you are on the right track to becoming a business owner. Your passion should be in first place, and then the money will follow.

I am not saying it is not feasible to start a business only to make money. You can do that, but it will work during only a short period of time. The reason: when you don't have passion, chances are you will tire of your business and won't feel like doing what you have to do to accomplish the goals. The business will fail sooner or later. Also, people won't believe you because they can sense when you are doing something only for the money. But when you are passionate about your business and truly want to offer a great experience to your customers, they will buy from you over and over again and will recommend your products and services to others.

Can you imagine the Russian tennis player Maria Sharapova starting her own business to sell candy? Well, that is exactly what she did, following her passion for candy!

Her business is amazing. Even if you don't like candy, which I doubt, you will feel like trying them all. It is easy to see her brand Sugarpova was born with passion. Sharapova's candies have beautiful and fun packages, unexpected shapes, and playful names to match.

Sharapova has won twenty-nine World Tennis Association (WTA) singles titles including all four Grand Slams, among several other titles. She was also silver medalist in singles at the 2012 London Olympics. And she is a real athlepreneur, using the same passion from the courts into her business. This is what Maria tells about Sugarpova:

"I've always had a sweet tooth. And I am not exaggerating one bit. My earliest memory of candy is being a little girl back in Russia and asking my parents for a lollipop after a good practice on the tennis court. It was that little treat I looked forward to. And here I am many years later hoping to get a sweet treat after a good practice. So when the name Sugarpova came about and I put the two together, I realized how much fun this could be. I have been a part of many projects, collections, collaborations, shoots, but at the end of the day I was always just that... a little part of it. So I put my thinking hat on and realized I wanted to start something on my own. Something that could bring the fun and passion of gummy candies to life and can be my own little project from start to finish"[1].

Sharapova's business website reflects all her passion for candy and for delivering a great experience to her consumers: sugarpova.com.

Passion is important because without it you are not able to offer the best experience to your clients. Results will not happen as you expected, and you won't have the energy to look for solutions or learn new things that can help you improve the business. Passion inspires the team working with you. But the lack of passion can do the opposite. Trying to open or manage a business without passion is, unfortunately, a common mistake with sad consequences. But you can avoid that!

Test 1: Take action now

Be honest with yourself and answer the question: Am I passionate about my business idea?

If the answer is a big and loud "yes," congratulations! You are ready to go ahead to the next test. If the answer is no, then stay calm and review your idea. This is a process that takes time, so don't feel frustrated if you need to give yourself more time. You will know you have something special when the new idea makes you smile only by thinking about it. You need to feel happiness, passion, and joy. You will be energized by the idea that comes from your heart. If you are not sure yet, and you need more information to help you get here, don't put pressure on yourself. Keep reading the book. You can always go back to this exercise and refine your idea.

TEST 2

Let's talk now about the second common mistake that we see in new businesses and why it is so important to check it in your feasibility test.

People also ask me a lot whether is true that they will work less in their own business than they would as an employee at another company.

The answer couldn't be more direct: no, absolutely not. Actually, you will work much more, compared to working a position as an employee.

I see a lot of people making this common mistake, believing that by becoming a business owner, the workload will magically decrease. It's not true. You are not on a vacation. You have responsibilities and deadlines, the same as you have as an employee. Especially during the first year of starting your new business, you will work a lot; you will work at night and on weekends.

But this is no reason to panic. To the contrary, if you are passionate about your business, you will also have fun as never before. When you are working on something that you truly believe in, you don't feel the time passing by. And if you have clarity about each task, none will feel like something that you are putting effort toward for no reason. You will work more, but enjoy every second. Bringing your business to the podium is worth every drop of sweat along the way.

Test 2: Take action now

Be honest with yourself and answer this question: Do I want to be a business owner just because I aim to do less work?

Okay, it is perfectly normal to wish to do less work. And no one is saying you should work like crazy and forget about your family and friends because you want to start your business. We all need to have a social life. We need to go for a walk, run, and dance. Whatever you like to do, you need to keep those activities in your life because they give you balance. We cannot be creative if we don't give our brains some time to rest.

What I want you to do here is be honest with yourself so you can avoid frustration. Because if, for any reason, you believe that by becoming a business owner, you will feel like taking vacations all the time, with a free agenda and no responsibilities, then you will end up seriously frustrated and with a business that will never score as it was meant to.

TEST 3

By now, you should have a business idea that you are passionate about and understand that becoming a business owner requires a lot of dedication. You are on the right track to having a business that will make you and your customers happy.

But how do you know if you will like the business you dream about?

Unfortunately, it is not possible to know that in advance, but there are some questions that you can ask yourself to get a better vision of your future as a business owner.

Having passion is not enough if you are not connecting this passion with something you are good at. This combination should move you towards the dreams you have for your life and future.

You will enjoy your business if it helps you reach your dreams. All the energy and effort you are putting into your business must guide you to a fulfilling as sense of purpose in your life.

Let's say you dream about becoming location independent. In this case, planning to open a business that needs a brick and mortar location will not help you achieve your dream. Even if you think about starting the business and keeping it for two or three years, you won't have the feeling of real accomplishment and, therefore, you will feel something is missing. This is not good for you, nor for the business. But an online business could fit perfectly for you. Choose something that you have experience with, something for which you know how to do the work, and think about how you can offer it online.

You are good at writing? How about offering newsletter creation services online? Don't waste your time and money on something that goes in the opposite direction from what you're dreaming of for your life or is not related to something that you are good at.

Test 3: Take action now

Think about a big dream you have for your life. Now connect this dream with your business idea. (Don't forget, your business idea should be related to something that you know how to do). How does it feel? If you are able to see how your business will help you reach your dreams through doing something you are good at, it is likely your business idea will become a successful venture and you will enjoy it a lot.

If you are not there yet, don't worry. All these tests take time, if you are taking them seriously (and you should, if you want to build a business that will make you feel complete and fulfilled). It is important to give yourself time now to evaluate all of these points before entering into the field to play as business owner. This will save you a lot of time and money, and you will avoid a lot of frustration as well.

TEST 4

Let's review what you have until now:
1. You are passionate about your business idea.
2. You are willing to work hard to make it happen.
3. You are using your skills in the business (and the combination of passion + hard work + skills helps you get closer to your dreams).

To finish this lesson and the feasibility test, let's check the last point.

Now you need to verify if you have customers. A business only exists if you know there are people out there who are willing to pay for your products or services. If you don't have customers, then your business doesn't exist.

You need to have clarity about the value that you are offering to your customer. Bear in mind that in order to have people willing to pay you, your offer should solve your customers' problems. Identify how you are going to help them, as well as the solution that you will give them.

As an example, let's imagine you offer catering services for events. Your value is not delicious food. What is the problem you will solve for your clients? Delicious food for people attending your customers' event, so they don't need to be concerned about whether attendees will like the salad, how many cupcakes they should have per person, or if the food will be there on time. By hiring your company, they will forget all about it and focus on the main purpose of their event, which is not the coffee break, right?

Ask friends, send a survey to your contacts, talk to people whom you believe are possible customers. The question should be simple:

Test 4: Take action now

"Would you pay for this product or service?" Ask as many people as possible. Remember to ask only for the ones people whom you believe are in your target audience. If you want to offer newsletter creation services, don't ask people who don't have a business or a personal website/blog, unless of course, you know exactly how the newsletter will solve their problems.

You should see sparks in people's eyes when you talk about your offer. If you believe they are saying they would buy your product just because they don't want you to feel sad, then don't lie to yourself. It is better to make adjustments to your offer before moving ahead with your business. If you don't know yet how to make these adjustments, don't panic. There is an entire lesson about your ideal offer. Keep reading to get more clarity. You can come back here later.

"Talent wins games, but teamwork and intelligence win championships."

—Michael Jordan

(17 Feb 1963)

NBA website, under "Legends": "By acclamation, Michael Jordan is the greatest basketball player of all time."

6-time NBA champion; 5-time NBA Most Valuable Player; 10-time All-NBA First Team; 9-time All-Defensive First Team; 14-time All-Star; All-Star MVP; 2-time Olympic gold medalist; Basketball Hall of Fame, 2009.

LESSON 2

PARTNERSHIPS

Roles & Responsibilities Guide
to Creating a Golden Team

Do I need a partner?

Whether or not you need a partner in your business is a common doubt—and an important one. It is so easy to choose a dear friend or a beloved family member as our partner because "We get along so well that it would be impossible not to happen the same in business," right? Well...wrong.

Or sometimes you believe you cannot start a business without a partner because you don't have enough money to invest. This is not true either. A lot of people decide they need a partner to put money into the business before even analyzing how much money they will need, or worse, if it is necessary. In today's world, we have many tools available to help us to start a business, and many of them are free.

There are basically two reasons for you to have a partner (or partners) in your business:

1. You cannot take care of all the work by yourself.
2. The business requires more money than you have.

Let's look at more details about each one of these possibilities.

You need someone to split responsibilities

There are a lot of responsibilities related to your business, and it is natural that you won't be able to do all by yourself. Then you start to wonder if a partner would fit perfectly. And honestly, one would. That is true, you cannot handle everything and expect to have everything done and done on time.

But that does not mean you need a partner to own the business with you. You can hire employees, virtual assistants, or other companies to handle some activities for you. Never forget, people working with you—as employees or suppliers—are also an important component for successful business. They are your team. And no matter how talented you alone are, you need the team working together to win the gold medal. Even if you think about athletes, such as tennis players who compete alone on the court, runners, or golf players, they are all part of a team. They have coaches, nutritionists, physiotherapists, and several other specialists supporting them before, during, and after every game or race. Game after game, race after race. As Michael Jordan said, talent wins games, but teamwork and intelligence win championships. You can apply these ideas in everything related to business partnerships.

Some cases partnerships are born during conversations between friends. You have the same interests, and suddenly you have a great business idea together. The idea and the partnership are born together. It now feels like the business will not exists if one partner is not there. And this is perfect. You just need to be clear about who will be responsible for each task and build a partnership based on trust and honesty. We will talk more about it in a moment.

Tactical Plan 1: Splitting responsibilities—Take action now:

Imagine you are a tennis player and have a partner to play doubles. So you are playing together against two other players. Your team started the game already winning, and you are rocking. All you have trained to do together is working, you know when and where to move on the court, and you are scoring big time, like Serena and Venus Williams playing doubles at Wimbledon. Cool, right? Now imagine suddenly you both forgot all you have trained to do. You don't know if you should hit the ball or let it go to your partner. Then you decide to hit, and your partner decides the same thing. Both run to the ball, and you do that repeatedly, again and again. The result? Total disaster. Can you imagine Serena and Venus playing like that? Of course not, because they know exactly how to move on the court, making different moves in the game without blocking each other. Both play, have fun, and score.

There is a reason why we are doing this exercise: to develop a tactical plan so you will play, enjoy, and win as a team. If you don't have a partner, don't worry. The exercise will help you evaluate which tasks of the business should be 100 percent under your responsibility and which ones you should look for support with.

Draw a chart with one column for each partner in the business. If you are only two, make two columns, if you are three, then three columns, and so on. If you don't have partners, this exercise will be helpful for you as well. Make two columns. In case of two or more partners, I suggest you do this exercise together. It is interesting, and you will have much more clarity on how to split responsibilities in a fair and effective way.

You can also use the workbook to do the exercises from this Lesson. It is ready to fill in. Download your free bonus here: athlepreneur.tv/workbook.

Now, on a separated piece of paper, write down all activities related to your business. I will help you with suggestions:

- Product/service development
- Sales
- Marketing/communication
- Customer service
- Administrative tasks
- Cash flow control
- Contracts (writing & review)
- Business plan (I know. Don't panic. There is an entire lesson about it.)
- Main contact for suppliers
- Website content
- Social media updates
- Information technology

The next step is to put each activity in a column on the chart that you prepared or by using the workbook. If one partner is good in sales, than this task should go under her/his column. The partner who has finance skills should have cash flow under her/his column. By doing this, it is easy to see if a partner has more of a workload than the other partner. This exercise is like creating a tactical plan before the team enters the field. Now everyone should know what to do. And the entire team has visibility about who is doing what, making it is easier to work together.

If someone has too many activities under the same column, you need to review it and make sure no one has more than what he or she is capable of managing. The issue is not the ability to handle the activity, as you already divided them according to the skills in the group. The issue is more about how much is possible for each one person to deliver, knowing that each day will always have twenty-four hours. Even in a ninety-minute football match, players' performance will decrease when they need to keep playing overtime.

Keep in mind that you can always do the exercise again and update the columns. New responsibilities will come, and it is also possible that you will want to shift responsibilities between partners at some point.

In case you don't have partners, you will use two columns: one for you and another for "support." Under your column, you will put down all of tasks that you plan to do. Consider focusing on the ones for which you have better skills. If you are good in finding and managing suppliers, put this under your column. Now you know that you will dedicate part of your time to looking for new suppliers, hold meetings with them, negotiate prices, and check on how you can improve the business together. Let's say you don't have this skill or don't want to manage suppliers. Then put this activity under the column "support." Now you know you need to hire someone to do that, or you can even consider finding a partner with this skill so you can be complementary to each other.

Remember to check to see if you have too many activities under your responsibility. If this is the case, review what else you could remove from your column and put them under "support."

This exercise is valuable because it helps decrease the overwhelming feeling that usually comes when you plan to start a business. After clarifying the owner of each responsibility, it is easier to focus, and you won't feel the weight of all activities over your shoulders only. Even if you don't have partners, you will have clarity about whom you need to hire to support you or which abilities you need to seek in a possible partner.

You can also do the same exercise to split responsibilities related to pre-opening activities like finding an office (in case you need one), buying furniture, installing software, or contacting credit cards companies to negotiate fees.

One of the sports that I enjoy watching the most during the Olympic games is synchronized swimming. It requires so many skills, and the athletes are strong and precise. But for us, watching outside the pool, it seems as if they are dancing and as if the water doesn't offer any resistance. And it doesn't matter how difficult the movements are for them; the athletes are always smiling.

Synchronized swimming and business partnerships have a lot in common. The Brazilian Olympic duet accepted my invitation to share their experience, as partners in sports, and how they have been improving throughout the years.

Lara Puglia Teixeira and Nayara Figueira have been together in swimming pools since 2007. In 2008 they were already in Beijing, for the Olympic Games. They have several excellent results, among them the bronze medal at the 2011 Pan American Games and three gold medals at the South American Championship.

Now you will read a lot of precious tips to make a golden partnership in your business, and they come directly from the experts.

Nayara explains about synchronized swimming: "We make synchronized routines, the more synchronized the better, but we can create different movements that add even more beauty to the routines. The success comes from the combination of making all [the] movements together, but also making different ones that will lead to the same goal." It is not easy to perform like that, and at the beginning, when they started to work together, they had to learn a lot before becoming a golden team.

Lara tells more about it:

"We used to have small conflicts because we thought that we had to agree all the time, go towards the same direction and that was supposed to be simple and easy. No! Actually, it took us one year until we were able to understand each other, our differences, and the roles that each one could assume on the duet: activities related to sponsorships, media, our website...those ones I had more responsibility [for], and Nayara had more leadership [on/for?] the pool, the technical aspects, what we had to prepare before going to a championship, our daily tasks.... In small steps we were finding our way to work together.

"We are very different people that must be synchronized, and we had an enriching learning process. Each one of us is productive in a different time of the day. I used to arrive at the trainings already full of energy, early in the morning. For Nayara it takes more time to get at the same level of energy. But it doesn't mean that one is putting more or less effort than the other. It is just our biological clock that works differently. That has a huge influence in our work. We had to learn how to manage that. So from my side, I stopped talking all in one at 7:00 A.M. I waited until later to talk about our plans for the week. The same about Nayara. She knows that my energy will be lower when we train in the evening. At 8:00 P.M. I just think about going to sleep.

"We have learned together to find the balance we need to be in sync. We have learned that we could split tasks, responsibilities, understand our differences, and still move towards the same direction. If you don't learn how to do that, the conflict is inevitable, and this has a direct impact on the performance. You have to talk to each other; talk about what has been difficult or easy to you. We don't hide; we don't keep the conflicts or problems hidden inside. We expose them so we can solve them. We need to be flexible and one must help the other to improve when necessary."

Nayara adds: "We feel that we are responsible for each other. This is partnership. You have to help the other to improve because we want the best result as a team. If we don't do that, we won't have the performance we want".

They are a great example of a golden partnership, right? So now let's talk about another important topic: trust and honesty.

Tactical Plan 2: Building trust and honesty—Take action now

This exercise is also a good one. It makes you visualize your biggest dreams for your life and think about how your business will help you to get there.

As we saw in Lesson 1, it is key to relate your dreams to your business; otherwise you won't have the feeling of fulfillment. Remember, your business must be a powerful tool to bring happiness to your life. If you don't feel your dreams are getting closer to becoming a reality, it is difficult to have joy and fun while working.

Also, you will get stressed, feeling you are moving towards nothing. We don't want that! You are totally capable of finding the perfect business for you, the one that will move your dreams closer to becoming reality, day after day.

Now write down the three most important dreams that you have for your life at this moment. All partners should do that, in case you are not the only owner. Use the workbook.

For each dream, you will think about how the business will help you to or block you from getting there.

Because I know this can be hard, I will give you an example to make it easier. Unfortunately, we don't dedicate much time to thinking about our dreams, and sometimes it is as if we don't have dreams at all. This perception is not true. It is also not true that you cannot dream big. So dedicate as much time as you need to get to know your dreams better. You and your dreams must become best friends!

Let's say that your three dreams are to:
1. Buy a big house in a quiet neighborhood
2. Make an amazing two-week trip with your family once a year
3. Learn to play guitar

These are your dreams now, and maybe they will change in a couple of years, because you achieved them or because you saw that other things became more important to you. And this is how things should be. You have the freedom to always review and update your dreams. You should pursue what matters to you. And we always have new dreams that take the space left from the ones that became reality.

Now let's check to see if your business will help you to achieve your dreams. You need to ask yourself some questions to be sure your business won't block you from your dreams. Questions like these:

1. Buy a big house in a quiet neighborhood: are you opening your business in an area that is inside, close, or with easy access to a quiet neighborhood? Or as soon as you have enough money for the house, will it take you ninety minutes of traffic to go to work?
2. Take an amazing two-week trip with your family once a year: Does your business depend on your biggest effort during the same weeks that your spouse and kids are free to take a vacation? Or you are able to manage that?
3. Learn to play guitar: Most likely, you are thinking, "Hey, this is not that important; my business won't block me from learning to play an instrument." And you are right, it won't, unless—for your business to become profitable—you need to fill every hour in your agenda with clients and tasks in a way that you will always be too busy to stop for one hour twice a week and go after your dream.

So even if you think this sounds silly, give yourself time to think about how your business will help you or block you from achieving your dreams. If you realize something is blocking you, you can always make adjustments to find the right balance. You can use the workbook for annotations.

Now, how does this apply to partners?

If your partner has no idea that you want to take vacations during the same two weeks that he/she is planning to put the biggest effort into the business, the result, of course, will be a conflict between you. Or maybe your partner never mentioned that the place where your office is located will make her/him arrive late every day due to awful traffic. You don't need to open your entire life and dreams to your partner, but when it comes to things that will affect or can be affected by the business, you need to be honest and build trust.

Partners need to be aligned all the time and have clarity in dreams and expectations, even if your partner is a beloved friend from childhood. That does not mean, since you've known each other for so long, you don't need to align expectations. The business must make your friendship even more special, not ruin it due to misunderstandings.

As a practical example, imagine you and your friend opened a beautiful store to sell kids' clothes. Having only one store is enough for you, and it moves you closer to your personal dreams. To take care of this unique store makes you happy. But it is not the same for your partner. Only one store is not enough. She dreams about a franchise model. Her goal will move her in a different direction. While you will put all your energy into offering a unique experience for mothers who go to the store to buy products for their kids, your partner is putting her effort into developing the franchise model. At some point, you will have conflict. It is like being on the same team, but playing different games.

This exercise is a great tool to help you build a business that will bring happiness to your life. Think positively and be honest with yourself and your partners. The result will be a business that fits with your dreams. You will feel they are getting closer to becoming a reality. This is the most powerful fuel you can have to pursue your business goals, because they lead you to something bigger in your life.

You need a partner to invest in the business

As I mentioned in the beginning of this lesson, this is the second reason to have a partner. The business requires more money than you have.

In this case, you have some options to consider:

1. Review whether you can start the business with less money, something that you can afford without investors. You will start smaller and work on a plan to grow slowly but consistently. If you are able to wait until your business reaches the size you want, this can be an option for you.

2. If you already know that Option 1 is not for you and you are aware of how much money you need to start the business and keep it running until it is profitable, you can apply for a bank loan. (We don't cover any kind of loan advice in this book. I strongly suggest you investigate further with an expert in the field.)

3. Look for business angels. These are people who want to invest in new companies, usually close to where they live, in return for a small percentage of the business. They are not executives inside the company, but they share their knowledge, experience, and network, besides their financial resources, as they have previous experience and success in business. Usually, they don't have huge fortunes, and the investment is made for small business. This is not a philanthropic activity. The business angels will choose the ideas that have highest potential to become profitable and make a positive impact on society. They are called "angels" because they are not investing only money, but also knowledge and experience to increase the chance of success for the new business owner. (Same as for bank loans, this book is not a guide to help you get investment from business angels. You can look for angel groups on the Internet. Get in contact with them, and talk to other business owners who have experience with this kind of investment.)

In Lesson 8, we will talk about your business plan. This will help you understand how much money you need to start your small business and keep it running until it is profitable. It is not a complicated or complex process. You will list the investments needed and work on a basic sales plan. At the beginning, your investments usually are higher than sales, but later it changes, and sales are higher. The key is to find the balance to make it happen as soon as possible.

Let's work on your business plan first so you can feel confident enough to decide if you need to have partners to invest money in the business.

"To achieve in sports you first have to have a dream, and then you must act on that dream. The best athletes are those who truly enjoy what they are doing and display a tremendous amount of work ethic. They continue to persevere in spite of setbacks and never lose sight of their ultimate goal."

—Dianne Holum

(19 May 1951)

In 1966, she became the youngest person to compete in speed skating World Championships.

Before her 20s: 4 Olympic Medals; 4 World Championship Medals; 1,500 m Olympic record.

At age 21, she started her career as coach. She helped U.S. athletes win several gold medals in the Winter Olympic Games. In 1976, she was the first female coach to train female skaters at the Olympic Games. She was inducted into the International Women's Sports Hall of Fame in 1996.

LESSON 3

YOUR IDEAL OFFER

Products and services that score big every day

How do I choose the best business model for me?

First, let's clarify what a business model is. In a simple and basic explanation, your business model is how you make money in your business. You can make money through selling products or services. A product can be something physical that you sell or information that you offer packaged as courses, PDFs, webinars, or videos. And a service is something you do for other people and can be an action such as computer maintenance, or a creation, like website design, logo design, or dance classes.

The important thing here to remember is that the best business model for you is the one that you feel comfortable with and are able to deliver with quality.

Now we are going to work on your business idea and choose the best business model for you.

Let's use an example: yoga classes. You love yoga and are good at it, and people enjoy how you teach them. Your first idea is to offer private classes. You go to your clients' homes and teach them. You need to move around the city all day and this can be stressful for you (let's say you don't like to drive). In this case, to make your business model work in a way that is comfortable for you, you need to re-evaluate the plan. Are you able to offer fewer classes a day and increase the price? If the answer is "yes," then you have found a solution to spending time in traffic. If you are always in a hurry, and driving puts you in bad mood, you won't be able to deliver quality to your clients. You need to avoid that. Another option is to open a small studio so people will meet you there. You can use the space also to offer seminars and other events related to your clients' interests.

In Lesson 8, you will learn how to calculate the investment you need to make for both cases: private classes at home and in a studio.

Another example: wine is your passion. You are an expert, have taken classes, and traveled to learn more. You are the one whom friends ask about which wine they should buy for a special occasion. You love to help them, and although you already have certificate that proves your expertise, this has been only a hobby. Now you want to make your passion become your business. Your first idea is to open a store and sell an amazing variety of wines from all over the world.

My suggestion to help you define your business model is to ask yourself: "Do I really see myself doing this?" Try to picture yourself inside the store, talking to clients, offering wine options, and managing the inventory. If you don't see yourself in this picture, no problem. That does not mean that your passion cannot become your business. But you need to unlock another business model possibility using the same business idea. What about a service, instead of products? You can become a wine advisor and offer your services to restaurants or companies that plan events. You can prepare not only the menu options, you can also support restaurant owners to offer a special wine taste night. You will be doing something you enjoy while you are offering value for your direct clients (restaurants), helping them offer a unique experience for their clients (people who go to the restaurant–your indirect clients).

I chose to quote Dianne Holum in this lesson because I like what she said: "never lose sight of the ultimate goal." This is totally related to your ideal offer. How?

Let's talk more about it because it is really important. You are choosing your business model based on an idea that came from a passion and skills you have. The business will help you achieve the dreams you have for your life. You are willing to work hard to make all this happen. We will add now another key topic to the formula to start a business like a champion: the ultimate goal is to make difference through your offer.

Your ideal offer is the one that delivers real value to your clients. It is the yoga class that makes your clients smile, makes them feel much better after a stressful day, and helps them to become fit and relaxed. They enjoy the experience; they enjoy being with you. You care about them because your class has the ultimate goal of offering a unique experience. You guide them to become fully present in this one hour that they are dedicating to their physical and mental healthy. It is not only a yoga class; it is a special moment. If you forget your ultimate goal, you will forget the nature of your business, the reason why people will choose you instead of others. The ultimate goal is the true value that you want to deliver to your clients. By doing this properly, you are making a huge step towards a successful business.

Laird Hamilton is known as the guiding genius of crossover board sports and is largely considered the primary influence behind many surfing innovations, including tow-in surfing, stand-up paddle boarding, and hydrofoil boarding. *Surfer Magazine* has labeled Laird as "the sport's most complete surfer, displaying almost unnerving expertise in a multitude of disciplines, and flat out surfing's biggest, boldest, bravest, and the best big wave surfer in the world today, bar none."[2] (Go to lairdhamilton.com to know more about this amazing athlete.)

Laird not only rides waves of up to 70 feet/21meters, he is also a successful athlepreneur as an owner of several different businesses, all related to his passions: water sports and a healthy lifestyle.

One of Laird's businesses, Laird StandUp (lairdstandup.com), is a company that produces and sells stand up boards and paddles. SUP, or stand up paddle surfing, is know as a new form of surfing, although Laird has been practicing and improving it for many years.

Laird Hamilton was interviewed by *Transworld Business,* and when he was asked about how his story and recognition could help retailers sell more paddle boards, this is what he answered:

"I think it's good for the whole industry and I'm not speaking like it's an ego thing. It tells the authentic story which helps sell boards and get people on them. I think that's the biggest part of it. It changes people's lives sometimes—just the simple act of standing on a board paddling. In our world, it's part of who we are so we don't even think about it, but for some people when they get that relationship it's life changing. If I can change somebody's life just by figuring out how to make them have fun, that's pretty cool stuff. That's worthy of a life's work—if you can start changing hundreds, or even thousands of lives, imagine what we can do."[3]

The business was born because of Laird's own passion for stand up paddle surfing. And now he can share the same experience through his product offer. But it is not only about selling the boards; it is about the experience of having a great time surfing.

Your Offer Assortment

We will add more details about your offer now. Let's talk about your offer assortment, or the total number of options you are offering to your clients.

The Brazilian basketball player Oscar Schmidt is a good example of how you can prepare yourself and plan a sustainable growth to your offer, always delivering the best experience to your clients.

Oscar, also known as 'Mão Santa' (Holy Hand) in Brazil, is a retired player often requested as a motivational speaker. He is unofficially considered to be the all-time leading scorer in the history of basketball. He is also a record holder for the longest career span of a basketball player and was inducted into the Naismith Memorial Basketball Hall of Fame.

Armed only with his experience as an athlete, Oscar started to offer lectures in 1996. That was the moment his athlepreneur career started. It was after 2003, when he retired, that he was able to focus on his business as a motivational speaker. He divided his speech into two different lectures. He was doing all by himself. Then he realized that, with more support from experts in fields that he didn't know how to manage, he would become more successful. He hired the experts and increased his offer to seven different lectures.

Nowadays, Oscar has twelve different lectures, and each one is focused on a specific field of interest for companies looking for motivational speakers. He is clear about which content he will deliver in each lecture. He even has short videos on his website, giving more detail about the content, so clients know exactly what to expect from him[4].

This example shows us that you don't need to start your business with a huge offer. Focus on a small offer and, after receiving precious feedback from clients, adjust and expand your assortment.

You can check Oscar Schmidt website at oscarschmidt.com.br

Now it is your turn.

Do you offer a single product or service? What are the options? As an example, we will say you produce and sell cupcakes. Your assortment is twenty different flavors of cupcakes plus five special flavors that you offer for only big events. For these five flavors, you accept only orders above fifty units because they use a special ingredient, which you cannot store. As a result, you have to use all of the cupcakes right away.

There are two factors that I like to consider when evaluating offer assortments. Using the same cupcake example:

1. Profitability: Do you make money with this flavor? Or does it use an expensive ingredient that will make the final price too high for your clients?

2. Availability: Can you offer the twenty flavors during the entire year or do some of them have seasonal ingredients? Check to see—if you are not planning to have so many seasonal flavors— that your monthly menu will end up with just a few options.

A product that is beautiful, but won't make you money, shouldn't be in your offer assortment. The same holds true for services.

If you plan to build your business through products or services that are seasonal, you need to consider that your revenues during high season will need to cover the expenses for the low season as well. Or you need to include different options during the low season to keep sales happening. You can also explore different forms of distribution. If you plan to sell only bikinis, you will sell a lot during the summer. In the winter, you can look for clients located in areas with reverse seasonality. Your winter is their summer. So you keep selling throughout the entire year.

You can combine products and services in your offer assortment. This is fine; you just need to be sure you have all the tools to offer both. Your ultimate goal to deliver the best experience to your clients cannot suffer a negative impact from a huge offer that you are not able to control. If you don't have the tools to deliver quality in products and services, then choose only one. Ask yourself: Do I have all the people I need, the software, the hardware? If you don't have all, verify if you are able to buy what is necessary, hire the staff you will need to support you and manage all this.

You can combine the offer through another company, a partner. You sell computers; they offer maintenance. One recommends the other. You don't need to have all under your company. But if you can do that and are able to keep delivering quality and stay profitable, then it is fine to expand your product assortment and offer services as well.

Prices: How to charge for your offer

Before we go into more detail about how to charge for your products or services, I would like to comment on something important: to offer the lowest price is not always a smart strategy. Don't have your business based on only pricing strategy. You can attract clients, but that does not mean low prices will keep clients buying from you.

Here you have the two main price structures to consider:

1. **Profit on top of costs:** usually used for products. You calculate the total cost per unit and add the profit on top to arrive at the selling price. Remember to add costs for transportation, warehousing, taxes, insurance, raw materials, labor costs, packaging, and any other cost related to the product or service. After adding the profit to this equation, you need to check to see if you are not overpricing compared to similar offers on the market. In case of services, you cannot calculate as you would for a unit of product. But you will consider, as cost, all you pay to be able to deliver the service with quality.

2. **Average market rate:** You charge the same as your competitors or increase your price a little and offer extra benefits. This price structure is more common in service-based businesses. In this case, it is important to check to see if you will still make money and be profitable when charging the same as the competition.

With any option you choose to work on the pricing strategy for you offer, you must check to see if you are making enough money to cover all costs and still make a profit. Otherwise you won't be able to keep your business running.

The Competition

All businesses have competitors. And this is good because competitors make us put forth more effort to improve our business. You want to win the game, be the first to cross the finish line, be the fastest, and have the best performance in your field.

To do that, you need to know your competitors. Don't work based on only what your competitors are doing. This is not healthy for the business. You don't want to be like them. You are unique. But you cannot close your eyes and ignore that competitors exist.

Your direct competitors are the companies offering the same kind of product or service and reaching the same consumers. If you have a restaurant, for instance, your direct competitors are other similar restaurants in the neighborhood or with easy access to get there. Your indirect competitors could be food delivery services or even the movie theater across the street. They include anything that makes your costumer change his or her mind and go to a different place, different from yours.

Spend some time checking your competitors, and do that from time to time. If you have strong competition, you might think of booking weekly time to take a look at what they are doing. As I mentioned before, this should not guide your business. However, you want to avoid offering the same things or losing clients due to an interesting offer from the competence. Remember, just because your main competitor is selling a new product or offering a new promotion, this not means it suits you well. Maybe the new product is unprofitable or the promotion is not working. Be unique and creative in a way that is good for your business and makes your clients happy.

Your Ideal Offer: Take action now

In your workbook, answer the following questions:

1. What is your business model: products, services, or both?

2. What is the ultimate goal of your business? The true value that you want to deliver to your clients? The unique experience that will make them smile?

3. What is your offer assortment? Consider profitability, availability, and seasonality.

4. Who are your direct competitors?

Some points to verify about your competitors: what value are they offering to their clients? Also: their strengths, weakness, suppliers working with them, consumers (are really the same as yours? how they differ?), how they promote themselves, what is their offer, how many people are working on the team, their prices, what people say about them, distribution channels they use and any other information you find relevant to check.

What is your pricing strategy? Start to make annotations.

In the next lesson, we will talk more about your ideal customers and why it is so important to know exactly what they want.

"It's not the will to win that matters—everyone has that. It's the will to prepare to win that matters."

—Paul William "Bear" Bryant

(11 Sep 1913 – 26 Jan 1983)

American college football player and coach.

6 national championships; 13 conference championships as Alabama's head coach. Upon his retirement, he held the record for most wins as head coach in collegiate football history with 323 wins.

LESSON 4

YOUR IDEAL CUSTOMER

Get to know whom you play for,
and fill the arena with raving fans

Who is my ideal customer?

When we think about the ideal customer, or to whom we will sell our products and services, it is common to think first about the demographic characteristics like gender, age, location, and level of instruction. This is great, but this kind of information alone won't tell you who your ideal customer is.

You need to know more than that. You need to have clarity about what your customer wants. In the previous lesson, we talked about your ultimate goal of offering true value for your clients. If you have only information like where your client lives, gender, and age, this is not enough to understand why they will buy from you.

Think about how you decide to buy a product or service. You have a problem, and you need help to solve it. Let's use a practical example. Maybe it is too dramatic to say "problem" for the need of buying flowers, but let's define it this way just for the explanation.

The problem you need to solve is not the act of buying flowers. You buy flowers because you want to offer them as a gift for someone; you buy flowers because you want your home to be beautiful; you buy flowers for inspiration, to make a beloved one smile.

So if you are selling flowers, you need to have all these thoughts in mind, all the reasons that will lead people to buy flowers. Then you have the demographic data. Do they live in the neighborhood? Do they come walking, maybe with the dogs, by car?

By knowing them better, you are able to offer a better experience to your clients. If you see that a lot of people stop by when they are walking their dogs, you can offer a nice area outside where they can sit for a while and the dogs can drink water. If you have clients buying flowers to decorate their homes, you can have a mural with inspiring pictures of how to place them at home. You can offer beautiful cards for the ones who are buying flowers as gifts.

So you see, you may have different types of consumers with the same problem to be solved. If you are able to solve the problem and offer a unique experience, they will be back.

Unfortunately, a common mistake is to try to attend to all the types of consumers whom you believe could buy from you.

Yes, a lot of people can buy from us, but if we don't choose whom we want to focus, then we won't be able to offer true value and quality. And there is a big chance that the same communication/advertising, and distribution channel won't work for all consumers you want to reach. Can you afford to have different marketing campaigns or distribution channels to reach all the people you want? Probably not, not just because of the investment, but also because a business needs to a have a focus to succeed. The advice here is to focus, choose one niche, and offer the best experience to this consumer.

I had the pleasure of interviewing a successful athlete who is also a successful entrepreneur, a real athlepreneur. Fabiola Molina is a Brazilian swimmer who participated in three Olympic Games, eleven World Championships, won six medals in the Pan American Games, and forty-nine medals in World Cups (fourteen were gold medals). She broke twenty Brazilian records and nineteen South American records. Fabiola has won more than 1,000 medals in her career, so she really knows what an athlete needs in the pool. Because of that, she saw a huge business opportunity and decided to focus on a specific consumer.

Fabiola launched her own business in 2004, offering swimsuits for athletic and casual use. Although she offered several models, she focused on a specific one, the sunkini. A sunkini is a two-piece suit, like a bikini, but designed in a way so you are able to train wearing it. The sunkini is confortable and won't move while you swim. Athletic women know how important this is in the pool. In Brazil, it is common to swim in outdoor pools, under the sun. The sunkini is designed with thin straps, so you will get tan as if you were wearing a bikini. Another great feature is the fashion aspect of her line: beautiful colors and graphics, much more feminine than the common black or navy blue swimsuits that used to be the only options available on the market.

No one was offering this kind of product in Brazil, and Fabiola knew it had big potential. To avoid taking risks that she couldn't afford, her strategy was to start small and grow the business as her sales increased.

Production got started only after sales were closed. Due to that, Fabiola was able to control her business and scaled the production in small steps. From a staff of three in 2004, her team has grown to twenty-two people in nine years of business. By focusing on offering the best experience for women to train in outdoor pools, plus having a careful plan to increase sales and production, she developed a successful business. Later, we will see more details on how she plans and controls sales goals and production. Today, members of the Brazilian Swim National Team wear her products, and she exports to several countries. You can check her beautiful collection—or "beautipool" as the slogan says—at the website fabiolamolina.com.br.

Fabiola knows her clients, and she never stops seeking improvements in the fabrics and design. She listens to her consumers, so she knows how to solve their problems. This leads us to another important topic.

How do I stay up with the needs of my customers?

There is no magic here. You need to be in constant contact with your customers. You need to visit places where they go, both online and offline. Talk to them in person, on the phone, through your blog—it doesn't matter how, but be in contact and listen to what they have to say. Be open to listening about what they like and dislike, so you will always know what they expect from you.

To take time to know and understand your clients is part of the preparation to win. You will never develop a fantastic product or service without listening to the people who will use it. You must have the will to prepare to win, as Paul "Bear" Bryant said. Preparation is key, and this is why I decided to quote him in this lesson. Bryant knew what he was talking about. He retired as head coach holding the record of 323 victories in collegiate football history.

Be in contact with your clients throughout the entire year so you will know if their needs are changing and when they change. Let's imagine you offer guided bicycle rides. People love your passion and enthusiasm to show the city. They exercise and learn more about the city history. They bring friends, recommend you, and always come back to ride again. But after a few months, your clients are no longer coming. You were happy they were always coming back, but now, for some reason, they are gone. You didn't pay attention to their needs when they asked to be guided along different routes. They were not tired of you and your energy and passion. They just wanted to see different places.

Save time in your agenda to listen to your clients. You will find out about other business opportunities, and they will always come back wanting more. If you can solve your clients' problems repeatedly—with passion and quality—you will have an arena of raving fans.

There are dozens of ways to stay in contact with your ideal customers. You can create surveys, call them, or email them to ask about their experiences with your product or service. If you have an online store, you can surprise them and deliver a personal note together with the product.

We will close this lesson with an exercise that will help you find out more about your ideal customer. But before that, I want to comment about a question that I hear from people starting small businesses and also from people who already have one. It is a good question, so I want to share it with you.

<u>Is it possible to change my ideal customer?</u>

Yes, of course. I will not say this will be easy, but it is possible. You need to keep in mind the thought that the actual structure of your business was thought up as you first planned to attend to your ideal customer. The visual identity for your business is important as well. (We will talk more about visual identity in the next lesson). Most likely, you won't be able to use same name, logo, offer assortment, communication, and distribution plan for the new ideal customer. You will have to ask yourself if a transition inside the same business is possible or if the best option is to start a new business.

In the case that it is possible to keep the same company, you need to be sure to communicate the change properly. You will also work on a transition plan, so you can shift the revenue achieved with the old ideal customer to the new one.

Your Ideal Customer: Take action now

In Lesson 3, you specified the true value that you want to deliver to your clients and your offer assortment. Now we will take a deeper look at whom your ideal customer is. These two lessons are related, and you will see that by knowing your client better, you will be able to fine-tune your offer if necessary. This is great. Don't be afraid to make adjustments; they are positive because the plan is to deliver a better experience to your clients.

I like the following exercise; it is fun. After completing it, you will get the feeling that you know your customer better than anyone.

Use your workbook to answer the questions about your ideal clients below.

1. List the demographic information about your ideal clients: location, age, job, level of instruction, gender, number of family members, etc.

2. Where you can find your ideal clients online? Which websites, blogs, and social media sites do they visit? And offline? Where do they go?

3. What kind of magazines do they read—sports, comics, photography, science? What is their style—fashion, classic, sportive?

4. How they can contact you before they become clients—website, blog, email, phone, in person, Skype, social media sites, chat?

5. How they can get in contact after they buy from you—website, blog, email, phone, in person, Skype, social media, chat?

6. How do you plan to listen to your consumers—website, blog, email, phone, in person, Skype, social media sites, chat, by reading the same magazines, visiting the same blogs, going to the same places they go?

Look for not only the above information; go deeper. Read the magazines they read, visit the same websites, and sign up for the same blogs. By doing this, you will get to know your clients much better. Use all you have learned during this research to evaluate your offer assortment. Don't be afraid to make adjustments if necessary. You are improving not only the business, you are turning clients into raving fans.

"It is easier to do a job right than explain why you didn't."

Martina Navratilova

(18 Oct 1956)

Czech-American Tennis Player and Coach.

Among several victories in her career, she won 18 Grand Slam singles titles, 31 major women's doubles titles (an all-time record), 10 major mixed doubles titles, reached the Wimbledon singles final 12 times (9 consecutive years: 1982–1990), won the women's singles title at Wimbledon a record 9 times.

She accomplished a career Grand Slam in singles, women's doubles and mixed doubles. She is the only athlete to have won 8 different tournaments at least 7 times.

LESSON 5

VISUAL IDENTITY

You will wear this uniform every day, so make it right since the first game

Is it okay to start my business using a temporary logo?

Unfortunately this doubt arises more often than you can imagine. I say "unfortunately" because temporary logos always generate a huge amount of extra work and extra investment. Then people realize the importance of doing it right from the beginning when they need to pay a designer to "fix" the problem later.

As Martina Navratilova said, it is easier to do a job right than explain why you didn't. If you start working with a temporary logo, sooner or later you will have to update it. It will cost you money—not only to create the new one, but also to update all materials (business cards, website, receipts, newsletters, advertising) and to communicate the change to your clients.

Due to lack of money to invest, inexperience, or several other reasons, new entrepreneurs sometimes decide to leave the logo for later and use something temporary until they are able to update it. But when you open your business with a temporary logo, it relays a message that it is not good for the business; it is as if you deal with everything on a temporary basis, with no proper attention. It's not professional, and it is not healthy for the business.

In this lesson, we will focus on not only the need to have a proper logo, we will do better than that. We will talk about how to develop the best visual identity for your business.

Visual Identity, the complete package

You can think about visual identity as the uniform for your business—like a football jersey, from which people recognize the team, and the team is proud to wear it. It is easy to relate the yellow jersey with the Brazilian National Football Team, right? They are recognized by their uniforms, and other teams know what to expect when they see the yellow jerseys entering into the field. What about All Blacks, New Zealand's national rugby team, with their black uniform and the Haka performance? The jersey shows the team's values. Jerseys are iconic.

It is the same for your business. You want people to recognize the value you will deliver to them as soon as they look at you. So it is not about the logo only. Visual identity is a package that contains the name, logo, colors, fonts, and how to apply all this in your communication.

This is why I recommend hiring an expert to create the visual identity for your business. A good graphic designer will create a complete package that represents the values of your brand, the values you want to deliver to your clients. And a graphic designer will do that faster than you (unless of course you are one). And the designer will also verify details that usually we don't even think about: Is this file correct to print? Are colors on the computer screen aligned with colors to print? Have you ever printed something that on paper looked completely different from your computer's screen?

Then you know what I am talking about. A designer should check that in advance and make proper adjustments, so you will have consistency in colors. This is just one example to illustrate the importance of hiring an expert.

What do I need to consider to have the best visual identity for my business?

Names and logos must be easy to remember, speak, read, and write. Together with colors and fonts, they must represent your business values.

The twenty-two-time Grand Slam champion, American tennis player Venus Williams, launched her own apparel collection, which connects style and performance.

Venus says that the difficult in finding clothes that allowed her to express herself on the court the way she wanted, and her fierce desire to motivate people to move their bodies, were the key elements in the creation of EleVen by Venus.

She gives more details on how EleVen was born: "Arming myself with a degree in fashion, I set out to create something that would represent much more than I could ever achieve on the tennis court: clothing that allows you to express your individuality, cultivate strength and confidence and makes you feel good every time you put it on. The name EleVen represents how I strive to live every day—that is, without limits. In our world, '10' is just another number, but EleVen is a lifestyle—it's about challenging your status quo, embracing positive change, and pushing beyond whatever is holding you back from living your ideal life. We all have stories about reaching seemingly impossible goals, especially in the face of fear and doubt. Being an EleVen is about making those stories the rule, rather than the exception. Ask yourself: 'what else is out there for me?' Not sure? Good. Get up and go find out. We've got your back."[5]

The beautiful values that Venus wants for her brand, plus her strength and determination, are all visible on the logo for EleVen. The brand is strong, easy to read, easy to apply on her products, easy to remember, and totally connected with the values that Venus wants for her business. Check out her beautiful brand and products at elevenbyvenus.com Look Good. Play Well.

Now I want to share a good example of how the same kind of business can have totally different visual identities if they have different values. Let's imagine you have a beautiful coffee shop. If you use colors and fonts that give the idea of "speed," people will see your shop as a place to quickly grab the coffee and go. This could be perfect if this is what your clients are looking for, delicious coffee to go. But if in the same coffee shop we use colors and fonts that bring the feeling of "cozy," your shop will be a place to stop and take time, enjoying a delicious cup of coffee while reading a book.

Let's keep using the same example of the coffee shop. I said logos must be easy to read. But why? Imagine that the same name and logo will be applied on the façade of your shop and also on the espresso cups— the same logo in different sizes. Is it easy to read them both? Cups are white, the façade is made of wood, and the napkins are yellow. The visual identity package must contain different color simulations for the logo, in case you need to apply it in different background colors. A black-and-white version should also be available. I don't recommend that you spend your time trying to figure all this out. It is better to hire an expert to work on that, while you use your skills to improve the business.

If you are focusing all your efforts on creating a product or a business that looks great on the outside, at the end you won't be able to succeed. Imagine an athlete who spends too much time cultivating his public image instead of practicing to improve the performance. You don't want to be this kind of athlete for your business. You want to be a successful entrepreneur, an athlepreneur!

The visual identity will also consider a suggested font for use in text. You don't need to use the same font for logo and text, but visual harmony between them must exist. You will use this font for all your copy and communication. It must be easy to read, without details that confuse the eyes. Your clients need to clearly understand your message.

The visual identity will give you something important: consistency.

You need to be consistent when communicating with your clients. When they see your website, business card, and newsletter, they immediately should recognize the same company and its values. You don't want to confuse them and show different colors and fonts on your communication. This is also why you don't want to have a business card with the new logo while your website shows the temporary logo. It confuses people.

Visual Identity Check List: Take action now

You don't need to be the expert, but you must able to explain what you want in a clear briefing, in case you hire a graphic designer to create the visual identity for your business.

Below is a checklist to help you. (Use the workbook to fill in the information.)

- Specify your offer. Explain what you are selling (Lesson 2) and to whom you are selling (Lesson 4).

- Which values do you want to show—speed, trust, care, friendship, modernity? List at least five values that are connected to your ultimate goal, from Lesson 3.

- List your biggest competitors so the designer can check the brands. The idea here is to avoid using the same colors or anything that could be considered a copy. You don't want to copy them; your business is unique and deserves a unique visual identity.

- Where do you plan to apply the logo? Include here any special place that you want to apply it, such as on cars, trucks, shirts, or bags. The designer will think about the most common areas to apply it, and you need to be specific in case you need something different.

When you receive the visual identity proposal back from the designer, remember to check:

- Colors: Must connect to the values and be unique for your business. (You don't want to use red if your main value is peace.)

- Name: Easy to remember? Easy to speak?

- Logo: Easy to read? Is it possible to apply it in small and big sizes?

- Background: Can you apply the logo on dark and light backgrounds?

- Font: Easy to ready? Connects with the values? (You don't want handwriting fonts if you offer solidity, like in construction business.)

Always ask the designer whom you are evaluating to create the visual identity for your business if you can see his or her portfolio. Ask for references. You should be able to recognize clarity about other brands from the portfolio. Does the designer seem to have innate skills in translating abstract characteristics into something visual? Is it easy to understand wants and needs from clients in the portfolio? If the answer is yes, this will give you confidence to hire this professional.

"There is a complete difference between training for a specific event and goal and just training."

—Michael Johnson

(13 Sep 1967)

American sprinter, 4-time Olympic track & field gold medalist; 9-time World Champion.

During his career, broke world records in 200m, 400m and 4 x 400m relay. Made history in 1996 when winning gold for 200m and 400m. Recorded the fastest time ever clocked by a human, running 23 mph en route to his 200-meter world record performance of 19.32 seconds.

He's held the 400m record since 1999.

LESSON 6

SALES

Break the record with business goals that are realistic, measurable, and achievable

How do I evaluate and choose a distribution channel?

A distribution channel is how your product or service will reach your ideal client. It can be through your own brick and mortar spaces, online stores, affiliate links on internet, events, a sales team visiting customers, wholesalers, etc.

The best distribution channel for your business is the one that offers the best shopping experience for your consumer and the best selling experience for you. Let's use an example to visualize that.

You design and sell dresses for women. You have your own store and also a website, and you sell directly to your clients. These are your current distribution channels: your own store and the online store. Now you want to expand the business, and you are checking the possibility of selling your dresses in other stores. In this case, you will have a wholesaler between you and the final customer. This is a new distribution channel for your business. You plan to choose stores that can offer a great shopping experience for their clients, like you do.

But what about costs? You cannot sell to a wholesaler at the same price you sell directly to the final client. It will cost you part of your profit because you need to decrease the price in a way so that the distributor can buy from you and also make money when selling to the final customer. Is it still profitable for you? Are you able to increase the units sold through this new channel so much that you will make more money than if you just keep the business as it is today? If you increase the volume, can you decrease production costs? All these questions will help you to define if you should use this new distribution channel or if the best option is to duplicate the actual channel (in this case, by opening more of your own stores).

Now, I will offer an example for services as business model. Remember the yoga classes from Lesson 3? We talked about two different distribution channels: private classes at your clients' homes or classes at your own studio. The best distribution channel will be the one that offers a great experience for your clients and also for you. Your clients might by happy to have you in their homes for classes, but if the commuting ruins your day and your mood, you won't have a good experience. Sooner or later, this will ruin your clients' experiences as well. So you might reconsider the option of having your own studio. Although it requires more of an investment, it also gives you the opportunity to offer group classes and seminars as a way to increase revenues.

Another important point to consider when planning the distribution channels is seasonality. We will see, in a moment, how seasonality affects your sales goals. Let's understand first how it affects the distribution channels.

Imagine that you have your business located in a country in Central America. You sell swimsuits through stores located on the beaches, and it is hot during the entire year. Even when it is winter, temperature won't drop much. It just rains more. It sounds like a paradise for your swimsuit business. But when rainy season arrives, your clients don't go to the beach. It is hot, it rains for only two hours, and there is the sun again. But your customers don't go to the beach because they consider the rainy season as winter. The result: they don't buy your products. The distribution channel is totally affected by seasonality, even in a tropical paradise. You need to look for new options that will help you increase sales during rainy season. So you do more research with final clients, and you find out they like to go to clubs in the city during rainy season. They go to indoor pools. Now you can explore a new distribution channel: stores located inside the clubs.

Your distribution channels are totally related to your sales goals because one doesn't exist without the other. Now we will talk about how you can plan sales goals that are realistic, measurable, and achievable.

Planning Sales Goals

Your annual sales goals are the result of how much you plan to sell every month, by distribution channel.

Your sales must be bigger than the amount you spend to keep the business running, otherwise it won't last much time. And we don't want that. We want you to have a business that is profitable, gives you the money and freedom you desire, and helps you achieve the dreams you have for your life.

This is why you should dedicate time to planning the sales goals. If you don't have a plan, then how you are going to pursue the results you need to keep the business alive, the same business that will help you achieve your dreams?

This planning is important, and I chose to quote Michael Johnson to open this lesson so you won't forget that. He said that there is a complete difference between training for a specific goal and just training. He is totally right. Goals give you the reason to go after the results. As an example: you need to sell 3,000 dollars monthly during a period of six months, using your regular distribution channel because this is the minimum you need to pay for expenses and keep the business alive.

The sales goals usually are planned on a monthly basis, but depending on the business you have, you can plan weekly goals or any other period of time that better suits your needs. If you have a restaurant, it probably will be better to have weekly goals because you are producing food and delivering it on a daily basis. And your inventory is perishable. You cannot afford to lose a lot of raw food because you didn't have the chance to cook it. With weekly goals, you can buy all the ingredients you need in the quantity that makes sense for your sales goals.

In this book, we will work with monthly sales goals. Also, keep in mind the idea that these goals must be realistic, measurable, and achievable.

Realistic: You are planning something so that it is feasible, considering the distribution channels, seasonality, and available tools you have to support your sales process.

Measurable: You have the tools you need to measure the results.

Achievable: What you are planning is possible to achieve. Not so low that you will miss opportunities for growth and not so high to make you frustrated.

Now, using the same example from the dresses store:

Realistic: Is the amount of money you plan to sell connected to the number of dresses you are able to produce and sell in your store? This is the goal for sales coming from the store. You are also planning to sell to wholesalers. Then you must be realistic about this new distribution channel. Let's imagine you will sell to a big department store. Are you able to produce and deliver on time? Does the volume you are planning make sense considering the number of stores that will offer your dresses?

Measurable: Do you have a system to register the sales you made? It can be a simple one, just an Excel sheet. Or it can be software that controls the sales and inventory. It doesn't matter how you will do that, as long as you have control over the real sales versus the plan. You must be able to compare the plan with the real results. This is an important thermometer to help you adjust the plans for the following months.

Achievable: You plan to sell more dresses for Mother's Day. This is achievable, considering seasonality. During Mother's Day week more people will look for gifts, and your product is a perfect one. But to achieve the sales you are planning, you must consider whether you have all the tools (in this case, the proper communication so you can remind your clients that a dress is a nice gift to their mothers). But if you plan a monthly goal that is too high, even using the correct communication, you will not achieve it, and it can be frustrating. Also, you will produce a lot of dresses that will increase your inventory and probably will be sold with discounts in the future.

Before we start with the exercises for this Lesson, I want to share some thoughts with you.

Take one step at a time so you won't feel overwhelmed. This activity is fun, and you will enjoy it. You are working on the initial plan, and you will make updates later. You will always review your sales goals to make sure they are aligned with reality. The market changes, new competitors arrive, some leave, you can be featured in a magazine or TV show, and suddenly more people look for your offer. Anything can happen. It is a dynamic process, and you will be need to be prepared for new opportunities. Don't be afraid to update your sales goals every time you feel it is necessary.

To encourage and inspire you, I will share what Fabiola Molina told me during our interview. You remember Fabiola and the sunkinis, from Lesson 4, right? She explained how she plans and follows up her sales goals:

"The business started small, just my mother and I, with our own investment. We don't work with outsourced production, so we first bought the sewing machines. You need three machines to produce swimsuits, sunkinis, etc. I didn't have the technical knowledge to buy the machines, nor to be a business owner. So I took courses to learn, and I asked a lot of questions to people that already had more experience than I did. I've learned that we always meet amazing people that are willing to help others to grow, when you go for your dreams, when you fight for what you believe. It is worth it to go after your dreams. It is not easy, but it is possible. I've met nice people that gave me precious tips, that told me important things, truly helpful.

"At the beginning, we only had one seamstress working for us. So our goal was to find a place where we could put the machines and also sell to clients. We rented a place, and it was just after we had the minimum structure to operate that we started to hire more people, and we hired three employees. We produce after we sell, and this was our strategy in the beginning to control the business. But this also means that you must go after sales, and the sunkini was a strategic product in our offer.

"We have monthly sales goals and an annual goal, and we are always following up on the business performance. We are very organized and always calculate everything in advance. If we know that with the machines and the number of employees available, we can only produce 1,500 units, then we will not sell 2,000. But if we want to increase the business in more 2,000 units, then we know how many machines to buy and people to hire. So our strategy was to grow the business in small steps.

"We also have goals for production. Those are divided into two daily goals: morning and afternoon. Without them, we would lose control of the business. Production goals and sales goals need to be aligned.

"Of course, it is not always that things work exactly as we planned. I never gave up when the monthly sales didn't reach the goals. Patience is very important, like in sports. Sometimes it seems that you are training, training, and training, but the results never show up. Then you have to stop and evaluate. What is wrong? You need to try a different path.

"I had to re-evaluate my career as an athlete several times. It is not because I had so many victories in my career that things always worked out perfectly for me. On the opposite, in several moments things were not happening as I expected, and I had to look for a new coach, move to a different country, different city, look for a new method of training, find out another way of improve my performance. It is the same in business. When results are not what you were planning you must ask, 'Why?' You must analyze and start again in a different way. Just because your idea didn't work, it does not mean that you don't have a future or the idea is not good enough.

"Sometimes you choose the wrong way of executing the idea. By searching for a new way of working, you will find something so much better than you could imagine. Perseverance is important; you have to keep trying new paths in business. Always be in search of the best one, of course.

"It is also important to have the team aligned. Same as in sports, everybody with the mission in mind. What is our mission as a company? Not only goals, but the mission as well. We have twenty-two employees, all women. We have meetings so we can maintain [the] same mood, objectives, everybody working aligned, knowing the 'why.' The 'why' is important because it gives you the motivation to wake up every morning and go to work. Like when you go training, and when it is not easy, you think on your motivation: I want to go to the Olympics. If I stay home, I won't improve my performance, I won't go to the Olympics. This is a huge motivation, go to the Olympic Games. So even if the trainings are really hard, it is so difficult, but they are worth, because of the motivation.

"So in my company, I want the team to know why they are working on their tasks. It helps the business to move forward. The team meetings are very important. I always want to hear how people are feeling regarding their work and what we need to improve. We have leaders on the team; they coordinate the activities and follow up the performance. You have to be opened to hear their feedback. Not only about production but also about people. If someone is acting in a way that is not positive for the group, we need to understand what is happening. We are all women on the team. We like to talk, so we talk about the attitudes that are causing the problem to identify it quickly and find the solution. The team leaders have weekly meetings scheduled. And once a month, we have an all-employees meeting. The weekly meetings help to steer the business; they are the gear that puts everybody on track, to go to the same direction."

For me, this is such a beautiful inspiration, how Fabiola started her successful business, always willing to learn, to improve and go after bigger goals, one step at a time with patience and perseverance. A real athlepreneur.

Take action now: How to use your workbook

In the workbook, you will see that months are named like: pre-opening, month 1, month 2, month 3, and so on until month 12, one column for each month, in a total of thirteen columns. Pre-opening is related to everything that will happen before you launch your business. Months 1 to 12 are related to a period of one year for your business since the first month that the business is running. If you started in March, just change "Month 1" to March, "Month 2" to April, and so on, until you have the entire year.

To plan the second year of your business, you will use Year 1 as the base model and then update it.

Now, let's start!

Monthly Plan for Events: Take action now

First you will work on the events that will help you know when to increase sales goals or when you should decrease them. You will do that on a monthly basis using the workbook. Just include the events on the correspondent month/column.

I will help you with an initial list:

- Christmas
- Valentine's Day
- Mother's Day
- Father's Day
- Back to School
- Halloween
- New Product Launch
- New Store Opening
- Try On/Tasting Activation (when consumers can try our products and services before buying)
- Sports Events (races, championships, any event that you are sponsoring and is connected in some way—maybe not directly connected, but your offer relates to the event. Example: Need nutrition advice to be prepared for "Your City Name Here" Marathon?)
- Expos & Fairs (with your own stand or through other people's stands)
- Teacher's Day (or any other professional celebration that relates to your offer)
- Sale/Discounts (This event usually drives traffic, but remember to consider that you will sell with discounts.)

- Religious Events
- Local Events (like Strawberry Month, Restaurant Week)
- Exhibitions (art, science, etc.)
- Seasons (Summer, Winter, Spring, or Autumn)
- Any other event you can include here that has relevance to your business. (Example: if you are a photographer for weddings, it might be interesting to check which is the preferred month in your city for this kind of event. For personal trainers, few months before summer can get pretty busy, since this is when people want to be in shape to go to the beach.)

It is important to remember that the same list will help you plan your production and inventory (in the case of products) and your agenda and resources (in the case of services). This list also supports you in planning what kind of extra resources you will need in terms of transportation, packing, staff, warehouse, etc. You want to always be prepared to meet the demand. Having a clear plan behind the sales goals will help you.

By the end of this process, you will see that some months don't have events. That is okay. Soon, we will talk about marketing and how you can create small events to fill in all twelve months. The idea for this initial list is to create a solid base for you so it will be easier to plan the sales goals.

Now you know in which months you can increase your target sales and also when to decrease them. This avoids a lot of anxiety and frustration. You don't need to worry every day about what you are going to create for the following week in order to sell more. You have a plan, you have focus, and you can use your energy for the tasks that will bring you results.

Distribution Channels: Take action now

Still using the workbook, you will fill in, below each event, which distribution channel you plan to use. You may use more than one per event. Just write down how your clients will have access to purchase your offer.

Here you have some ideas:

- Store(can be yours or not)
- Online store (can be yours or not)
- Pop-up store (temporary stores or itinerant stores)
- Wholesaler
- Studio (can be yours or not)
- Galleries/Museums
- Phone
- Affiliated links
- Restaurants (can be yours or not)
- Expos & Fairs
- Sales Team
- Any other distribution channel that you plan to use to sell your offer

Sales Goals: Take action now

Now it is easier to think about your sales goals. You know how each month should behave according to your initial list of events, and you know how your clients will buy from you (the distribution channels).

If you plan to distribute your products in restaurants, you can calculate how many restaurants you are able to attend in a one-month period, consider the capacity for production, and start from there.

(Number of restaurants) x (number of units each one can buy monthly) = sales goal

If you plan to sell to restaurants that are destinations for romantic dinners, you might increase the number of units close to Valentine's Day. But for restaurants that are destinations for lunch, Monday to Friday, you might decrease the number of units in a month with national holidays, when people usually don't go to the office.

The above examples are considering seasonality, as we talked previously about in this lesson.

Now, below each month, you will include how much you plan to sell.

If you offer products, calculate the number of units x average price (500 cupcakes x USD 2.50 = USD 1,250) .

If you have services, calculate the number of hours x average price (40 private yoga classes x USD 65 = USD 2,600)

Done with the twelve months? Excellent and congratulations! You just finished your sales goals. Now that you will be focused on specific goals, you won't be working too hard and crossing fingers, hoping to have a good month.

Remember, the goals must be realistic, measurable, and achievable. Now you have a better idea of how much your business can reach in a year, through monthly sales. In Lesson 8, we will work on the costs and expenses, so after finishing this book and all of the exercises, you will have a picture of how profitable your business can be, or how much money you can make.

"You can't put a limit on anything. The more you dream, the farther you get."

Michael Phelps

(30 Jun 1985)

American Swimmer.

Most decorated Olympian of all time, with a total of 22 medals. Holds the all-time records for Olympic gold medals (18), Olympic gold medals in individual events (11), and Olympic medals in individual events for a male (13).

Phelps is the long course world record holder in the 100m butterfly, 200m butterfly, and 400m individual medley.

LESSON 7

MARKETING

The 12 Laps Calendar:
make every month count

Why do I need a Marketing Calendar?

You already have your sales goals. Now you need to tell people you exist, so they can choose your business to help them solve their problems. (Remember, your ultimate goal is to help your clients through your offer).

In the same way you planned sales, you will plan communications. We are not focusing on the institutional aspect only. We will use the monthly plan that you already have for sales and start from there.

More and more people are looking for options using the Internet. So you want to have a good website. Don't waste your time and money thinking about complex websites. Unless your company operates through complex systems and databases online, you can use a simple website. This means your clients can easily find information about the company, products, news, and how to contact you.

The visual identity from Lesson 5 will be massively used in your marketing calendar. All your communications should follow the guidelines that you specified for your brand. Because of that, you will have consistency in your message, and it will be easier for your clients to recognize your business. When they see your website, business card, advertisements, digital banners, or social media—it doesn't matter what—they will visually connect them all and recognize your company, your business.

So you need a marketing calendar to help you reach your sales goals and also to have clarity about the investments related to communications and how they affect cash flow. You don't want to make the biggest investments during the wrong months or events.

The 12 Laps Calendar

In Lesson 6, you listed all the events that affect your business and that you can take advantage of. So now you can transform this list into your marketing calendar. You have twelve months for sales, and you will have twelve months for marketing.

I like to call it the 12 Laps Calendar because you will have clear monthly plans to tell the world your offer is awesome. You have twelve laps to do that, like in a race, and you want to make each lap count.

The 12 Laps Calendar is a live document, and you will update it any time you feel it is necessary. Don't be afraid to do that. A new opportunity appeared? You can include it. The fair you were planning to participate in was postponed? You will update the sales goals and the marketing calendar, no problem.

Remember that example for swimsuits and the clubs with indoor pools from Lesson 6? Imagine that a new club has just opened, and they have a store inside. This kind of store is part of your distribution plan. If you are successful during the negotiations, and if the new club will buy your products, you should update the sales goals for the upcoming months and also evaluate the marketing plan.

You will negotiate not only the sales, you will think also about how you will inform people your products are there. You can negotiate access to the email list from club members. Probably the club will not share the list, but they can send your email-marketing, inviting their members to go to the store and check your products. You negotiate to use their database as a win-win situation. By telling people about your products, they will sell more, which is good for them and also for you because you can start working on replenishment orders.

Your 12 Lap Calendar will look like this:

Lap 2 = Month 2 = April (if, for instance, you started the business in March)
Event: opening of new club
Distribution Channel: store inside the club
Sales Goal for this Lap: 30 swimsuits
Marketing Plan: send emails to members using The database from the club
Marketing Investment: email marketing design

Another example, from the cosmetics industry:

Lap 3 = Month 3 = May
Event: Strawberry Week
Distribution Channel: your online store
Sales Goal for this Lap: USD 6,000
Marketing Plan: promote in local media the

products that use strawberry as an ingredient
Marketing Investment: Public Relations (PR) agency

A PR agency can prepare a proposal for six or more months and search for opportunities in local media where your products could be featured (not only the products containing strawberry, but also other lines) during more months if you are able to invest in that. Otherwise, you can invest on digital banners as well, to be placed inside websites that are relevant for your clients. In Lesson 4, you listed all websites, blogs, and social media outlets where you can find your clients online. Contact them to know how much they charge for ads.

What if I have months with no events?

Don't panic, you will see that you have all the tools to help you be creative and include a new event. Remember that all twelve laps count.

We will work now with a reverse-engineering process. You were planning based on events. But if you have no events, you will see which tools you have available and transform them into new events.

How? I will share an example from the time I had my own sports brand in Brazil, selling apparel and accessories. There were months when we didn't have races, fairs, Valentine's Day, or any kind of event. The reverse-engineering process was simple to use. We had to ask ourselves: What do we have that we are not in use during this specific month? Answer: our assets, the sponsored athletes. Because there were no events to go to, the athletes were available. And our consumers were training for their personal goals in sports. We had several running clubs as clients because we offered athletic uniforms. So we called them to offer a benefit. Were they interested in having one of our sponsored athletes run with the group and share the experience after the training? Well, the clubs were more than happy to receive this free benefit from us. In exchange, they had to send our email marketing, which presented our products, and give us a space to expose our line and sell directly to the runners during the training sessions.

This simple system exercised our creativity and helped us achieve the sales goals, even in months with no events.

This is why I chose to quote Michael Phelps in this lesson. Because I want you to think big, to exercise your creativity, and not put on limits. The more you dream, the further you get. Make each month count for your business. Your business is helping you achieve your dreams, remember?

The 12 Laps Calendar: Take action now

Now, in your workbook, fill in the information in each month.

You will write down your marketing plan and specify the investment. Don't worry if you still don't know how much it will cost. Later, you can use these notes to ask for quotations. It is much easier and faster when you have a plan to base your request on.

Just write down all your ideas. I have a list here to help you:

- Paid advertisings in magazines or movie theaters, on TV or outdoor banners, etc.
- Digital banners
- Email marketing
- Phone calls
- Windows and in store communications
- Wholesalers' catalogues, magazines, and websites
- Blogs
- Social Media
- Public Relations
- Product Testing
- Seminars
- Any other idea that connects your business with your clients

Important Note about Internal Communication

Always keep in mind that everything you are doing to communicate to your clients must be informed internally within your company. This is important if you have employees or suppliers who are in direct contact with your clients. They must be aware of what is happening.

If you have an advertisement in a magazine, are exposing your offer at a fair, or have any other way of communicating or promoting your business to the world, you cannot afford to forget to tell it to your employees or business associates. Imagine a consumer calling to ask for more details on a promotion that you are doing in a shopping mall, and having the person who is answering the phone not know about it. It is not professional, and it affects your brand perception in a negative way.

Every single person involved in your business must know the values of your brand, what your offer is, and what and where you are communicating.

"I'm focused on what I want to do. I know what I need to do to be a champion, so I'm working on it."

Usain Bolt

(21 Ago 1986)

Jamaican sprinter, nicknamed Lightning Bolt.

First man to win 6 Olympic gold medals in sprinting and to hold both the 100 m and 200 m world records. Eight-time World champion, his awards includes the IAAF World Athlete of the Year, Track & Field Athlete of the Year, and Laureus Sportsman of the Year (three times).

LESSON 8

BUSINESS PLAN

Why you won't get to the finals without one

What is a Business Plan?

In this lesson, I will show you what a business plan is, how you can prepare a basic one, and why it is so important to have.

A lot of people want to run away when they hear the term "business plan" because it seems to be something complex. It is not. Remember, in this book we are talking about small businesses. When you write business plans for huge companies, then of course they will be much more complex. But don't feel overwhelmed. What you need to do for your business can be simple and effective. And you absolutely can do it. Some people are surprised when they realize they had all the tools to prepare their business plans, they just didn't know it yet. They needed someone to guide them during the process. And this is what I am going to do now.

The Business Plan is a summary of your business. It contains:

1. **Your business model:** How you plan to make money (your ideal offer). You already have this information from Lesson 3 Exercises.
2. **Your target audience:** For whom you plan to sell your offer (your ideal customer). You already worked on that on Lesson 4.
3. **Sales goals and distribution plan:** How much do you plan to sell monthly and where. This information is ready as well. It is your Sales Plan from Lesson 6.

4. **Marketing plan:** What you are going to do to communicate your business and reach your sales goals. This is your 12 Laps Calendar for marketing from Lesson 7.
5. **Expenses:** All the production costs and monthly expenses. Everything that you are paying for must be included in your business plan. Without this information, it is impossible to know if your business is profitable or where you need to focus to reduce costs and make the business profitable.

As you can see, your business plan is almost ready. If you completed all of the exercises from previous lessons, there is only one part that you need to work on to finish your business plan and become a new athlepreneur: the expenses.

Why do I need a Business Plan?

Simply put, you need a business plan to guide you, give you focus on what you need to do to become a champion, as in the quote by Usain Bolt. In your case, being a champion means to have a business that is profitable and leads you toward your dreams.

If you are looking for an investor, you will need to present a business plan. This is a powerful tool to prove that your business idea is worth the money to be invested.

Even if you are not looking for an investor, a business plan will show you how much money you need to start your business and keep it open until it reaches the break-even point (this is when you have recovered all money invested and the business pays itself with its own revenues).

Always bear in mind that the business plan is a live document. I advise you to check it from time to time and update it when necessary. Maybe you will have to include a new tax that didn't exist before, or perhaps the credit card companies have increased the percentage they charge you for each transaction received, or you need to account for an extra employee you hired, or add a new distribution channel that you opened.

Plan follow-up meetings to check and update your business plan. Don't wait until you have free time on the agenda. It is easy to procrastinate. If you always book one hour every two weeks to check the plan, you will see it is not complicated, and you will feel confident about seeing all of your sales goals and expenses on track. I personally like to check my plans once a week. It gives me clarity and focus.

If you have partners, plan these meetings together. Each one of you must be up to date on the business performance. Checking the business plan is an easy way to stay focused as a group and make decisions based on facts.

The Expenses: Completing your Business Plan

Below you have a list of several points you need to consider as expenses. In the workbook, you will find the same list, and you can fill in the information.

This list will help you to consider all investments to be made before starting the business and the monthly expenses as well. You will also review everything that you should consider as costs from your offer (products and services costs, like packaging, transportation, warehousing and taxes).

Regarding taxes and licenses, my advice to you is to talk to specialists. Make an appointment with an accounting office and a business attorney (ask your friends for recommendations). It is not worth it to try to find out all of this information by yourself. And it is overwhelming. An expert will tell you everything you need to know in one meeting. You need to check all taxes that you must pay accordingly to the type of business you have and the country/city where you are located. There are monthly taxes, quarterly or sometimes semiannual taxes, licenses you may need to pay, as in the case of businesses related to food. You will also pay to register your business's name and logo.

Your Business Plan: Take action now

Now it is time to research costs. You can use the workbook to fill in this information. You are almost there. Just one more step to have your business plan ready. One more step to win your gold medal.

Let's start with the list of investments you need to make before opening your business. Not everything on the list below will be part of your business. I included as many possible options as I could to avoid forgetting something. If an option doesn't apply to you, just ignore it and jump to next one (use the Internet and your contacts to research, appoint meetings, make calls). Fill in the information in the column "pre-opening expenses":

- Taxes to register your company
- Taxes to register name and logo
- Meetings with accounting specialist and attorney (Most accounting offices won't charge for the hour if you decide to keep working with them.)
- Hardware: computers, machines, and other equipment
- Software
- Courses to operate hardware and/or software
- Furniture and accessories
- Cleaning and painting
- Remodeling brick and mortar area
- Architecture plan
- Employees to support you on the pre-opening activities
- Travel expenses
- Telephone and Internet bills
- Visual Identity creation
- Website creation
- Website domain (buy www.yourbusiness.com)

- Website hosting service
- Staff uniforms
- Transportation
- Insurance
- Public Relations Services
- Any other costs related to pre-opening activities

Now the list of monthly expenses (fill in the information for twelve months):

- Rent
- Loans
- Repairs/maintenance fees
- Light and heat
- Internet and telephone
- Accounting services fee
- Taxes
- Cleaning
- Miscellaneous (office supplies, coffee, etc)
- Postage and packaging
- Bank charges
- Credit card charges
- Meals
- Transportation (gas & parking)
- Staff wages
- Insurance
- Website hosting service
- Website maintenance & updates
- Public relations services
- Assets (athletes, celebrities, anyone who you plan to invest in in exchange for testimonials)
- Pro labore (wages for owners)
- Any other costs related to monthly expenses

After completing the exercise for all months, you will have a picture of all expenses (all you are paying per month) and also all money that you will receive from your clients. The difference is your profit. You should be able to review this information on a monthly basis and the total per year.

Time to celebrate!

You made it! Congratulations, you won your first gold medal in business. You are an Athlepreneur!

Your business plan is ready. Now you are able to see how much you need to invest to start your business, you have an estimated value for monthly expenses, and you have sales goals that are realistic, measurable, and will bring profit to your business.

Transforming all you have done until now into a simple equation, you will have this:

(Money In) – (Money Out) = Profit

or

Sales – (products and services costs, monthly expenses, marketing investment) = Profit

If you are not reaching the profit you expected, use your business plan to look for improvements. Is the monthly rent too expensive? Should you increase the sales goals for the products with higher profit? Do you have the right distribution channels to do that? Is there some extra opportunity to increase sales that you can consider for your marketing calendar? Is there any month that you had a loss instead of profit? What caused that?

Remember, it is possible that you won't have profit in the first months after opening your business, depending on how many investments you had to make to be able to start it. You must read your business plan by each monthly and annual period. It does not matter if you have a loss or profit on a monthly basis; you will always carry forward the result to the following month. At some point, the negative numbers will turn into positive ones, until you reach the break-even point and start to make money. This means you have covered all the investments done and the business is now profitable. This can be fast or can take several months, depending on the kind of business you have and the results you are achieving.

Take advantage of your business plan and really use it to improve your business. Make it a solid plan that you can rely on. It must give you focus to operate with quality and be profitable. Dedicate time to work on your sales goals and follow up the results. Make adjustments when necessary.

The business plan must give you clarity on how much time you need to wait until the business is profitable. If you plan to leave your job as an employee to become a business owner, the business plan will help you calculate how much money you should save in order to keep your company running, until you start to make money through your products and services.

Don't forget to consider your personal bills as well. Not only must the business keep running, your personal life comes first!

I hope that by now you no longer have the overwhelming feeling that is so common when we decide to start a business, especially when you are doing it for the first time. I hope I was able to help you gain all the confidence you need to take action. If you are happy with the results, please leave a review on Amazon so you will help others to decide if this is the right book for them as well.

You can always contact me through my website. I will be pleased to receive your message. Please let me know if there is anything you suggest to improve the content in this book.

I invite you to go to athlepreneur.tv and sign up for free trainings and receive more information about my new products and courses.

I wish you great success on your journey to win more gold medals in business. Don't forget, you are an athlepreneur; you have inside you all the tools you need to be a champion!

CREDITS

Quotes from athletes in the openings of Chapters 1 (Emil Zátopek), 2 (Michael Jordan), 5 (Martina Navratilova), 6 (Michael Johnson), 7 (Michael Phelps) and 8 (Usain Bolt) from brainyquote.com

Quote from Dianne Holum in the opening of Chapter 3:
sportpsychquotes.wordpress.com/tag/dianne-holum/

Quote from Paul William "Bear" Bryant inn the opening of Chapter 4:
http://www.keepinspiring.me/100-most-inspirational-sports-quotes-of-all-time/

Websites mentioned on this book:
fabiolamolina.con.br
laraenayara.com.br
lairdstandup.com

1 Maria Sharapova about Sugarpova:
sugarpova.com

2 Laird Hamilton biography from:
lairdhamilton.myshopify.com/pages/laird-hamilton-bio

3 Laird Hamilton interview for Business Transworld:
business.transworld.net/112576/features/laird_hamilton_stand_up_paddle_surfing/

4 Oscar Schmidt about how he improved his lectures:
oscarschmidt.com.br

5 Venus Williams about EleVen by Venus:
elevenbyvenus.com

Recorded interviews:
Fabiola Molina – September, 20, 2013
Nayara Figueira – September, 27, 2013
Lara Puglia Teixeira – October, 2, 2013

ABOUT THE AUTHOR

Laura Brandes is a business strategist with more than seventeen years of experience, ten of them working in the sports industry for brands such as adidas, Reebok, Nike, and Speedo. A successful entrepreneur and passionate about all kinds of sports, she created and managed her own sports brand in Brazil.

Laura is the founder of Athlepreneur TV, an online channel and blog dedicated to help aspiring entrepreneurs gain confidence and reach their dreams through running solid businesses.

Laura has a degree in marketing and publicity and is a post-graduate in customer management. She speaks four languages and has international working experience on three continents. She is currently living in Panama.

Visit athlepreneur.tv to contact Laura and receive information about her new books, business coaching services, online courses, and seminars.